THIS JOURNAL BELONGS TO:

Made in the USA
Monee, IL
24 November 2021

82969751R00063